Christmas Preparations

A Christmas Pageant
For Youth

Cynthia E. Cowen

CSS Publishing Company, Inc.
Lima, Ohio

CHRISTMAS PREPARATIONS

0-7880-0098-5 PRINTED IN U.S.A.

This program is dedicated to the Sunday school staff at Grace Lutheran Church of Pembine, Wisconsin, who have faithfully used my materials and presented their programs to the glory of God. Their love and commitment to sharing the love of Christ through their Christmas programs has enriched their youth and challenged adults.

Christmas Preparations
A Children's Christmas Program

The Congregation Is Prepared

Welcome — Pastor

Narration

***Carol:** "It Came Upon The Midnight Clear"

(Grade 2, The Israelites, enter)

Time To Prepare The Community

Narration

Reader: Micah 5:2

Grade 2: "O Little Town Of Bethlehem" (vv. 1 & 2)

Narration

Congregation: "O Little Town Of Bethlehem" (vv. 3 & 4)

(Grade 2 departs and the Animals of Pre-K and Kindergarten enter)

Time To Prepare Our Homes

Narration

Reader: Luke 2:1-7

Pre-K and Kindergarten: "Away In A Manger"

Narration

Congregation: "What Child Is This?"

(Pre-K and Kindergarten depart and Angels of Grade 3 enter)

Time To Prepare Our Greetings

Narration

Reader: Luke 2:8-14

Grade 3: "The First Noel" (vv. 1 and 2)

Narration

Congregation: "The First Noel" (vv. 3, 4, and 5)

(Grade 3 departs and Shepherds of Grade 5 enter)

Time To Prepare Our Tree

Narration

Reader: Luke 2:15-20

Grade 5: "Go Tell It On The Mountain"

Narration

Congregation: "Angels We Have Heard On High"

(Grade 5 departs and Grade 4 Simeons and Annas enter)

Time To Prepare The Faithful

Narration

Reader: Luke 2:25-38

Grade 4: "Oh, Come, All Ye Faithful"

Narration

Congregation: "Infant Holy, Infant Lowly"

(Grade 4 departs and Grade 6 Kings enter)

Time To Prepare Our Gifts

Narration

Reader: Matthew 2:1-12

Grade 6: "We Three Kings Of Orient Are"

Narration

Congregation: "Good Christian Friends, Rejoice"

(Grade 6 departs and Grade 1 Marys and Josephs enter)

Time To Prepare Our Hearts

Narration

Reader: Matthew 1:18-25

Grade 1: "Silent Night" (vv. 1 and 2)

Congregation: v. 3

Narration

Congregation: "Oh, Come, Oh, Come, Emmanuel"

(All children return)

Time To Prepare The World

Narration

Reader: Acts 1:3-11

Children's Chorus: "Joy To The World" (v. 1)

Narration

***Christmas Prayer:**

ALL: **Lord Jesus, thank you for this time to prepare for your birth. Almighty God, we receive the gift of your Son who was born for our salvation. Pour out your Spirit that we may go forth from here today singing our joy and proclaiming the wonders of your love. Be born again in us this Christmas day. Amen.**

***Benediction:**

P: May the Child of Bethlehem bless you and keep you in his love and grace from this day on until his return. Go in peace and serve the Lord.

C: **Thanks be to Jesus, the joy of our world!**

***Congregation:** "Joy To The World" (vv. 2, 3 and 4)

(Children all depart)

(Offering may be placed in the plates in back.)

*Congregation please stand

Christmas Preparations

A Children's Christmas Program

The Congregation Is Prepared

Pastor:

Welcome to our children's Christmas program, "Christmas Preparations." As we continue our Advent journey, we pause at this Advent moment with our young people who have done a lot of preparing for you today.

Sunday School Superintendent or Other Leader:

Christmas Day is almost here! Are you ready? Have you made all your preparations to celebrate the birth of the Baby Jesus? Come and join us as we look at some of the preparations our Sunday school has made to help us remember that Jesus is the reason for this season. Join us by remembering that first Christmas so long ago with the singing of "It Came Upon The Midnight Clear."

***Congregation:** "It Came Upon The Midnight Clear"

(Grade 2 enters dressed as Israelites and carrying road signs "To Bethlehem.")

Time To Prepare The Community

L: God is always preparing his people. His plan of salvation was proclaimed through the prophets. Israel looked forward to the arrival of their Messiah. God even foretold where the Savior would be born. Hear from the prophet Micah.

Reader: Micah 5:2

Grade 2: "O Little Town Of Bethlehem" (vv. 1 and 2)

L: The community of Bethlehem was unaware that its Savior was born that first Christmas night. The Baby Jesus came to a people who looked forward to the birth of the Savior, but who really were not prepared. As Jesus stands in our midst today, the Spirit speaks to us as a community asking this question through our children:

Children's Chorus:
"Are You Prepared To Receive Jesus?"

Congregation: "O Little Town Of Bethlehem" (vv. 3 and 4)

(Grade 2 departs and Pre-K and Kindergarten enter dressed as animals. May carry face masks of a variety of animals as costumes also. Teacher may carry the manger with hay and place it before the audience.)

Time To Prepare Our Homes

L: Christmas is a special time when we decorate our homes in preparation for the holidays. We trim a tree and hang our stockings. Lamp posts become giant candy canes. Garland and lights are strung on the eaves and railings outside. In the midst of these elaborate preparations, we should pause to remember that the Christ Child entered our world in a very humble manner. His mother rode to Bethlehem on a donkey and then could find no place to stay. Hear what the gospel of Luke tells us about Jesus' first home.

Reader: Luke 2:1-7

Grade Pre-K and Kindergarten: "Away In A Manger"

L: A stable was prepared by God to house his precious Son. A manger was the crib that Mary placed her baby in. As we have prepared our homes for Christmas Day, we need to prepare our hearts to house the Christ Child. As Jesus stands in our midst today, the Spirit speaks to our hearts asking this question through our children:

Children's Chorus:
"Are You Prepared To Receive Jesus?"

Congregation: "What Child Is This?"

(Grade Pre-K and Kindergarten depart. Grade 3 enters dressed as angels.)

Time To Prepare Our Greetings

L: By now most of us have written out and mailed our Christmas cards. Notes of greetings to family and friends near and far are part of our Christmas preparations. Mail carriers speed our wishes for a blessed Christmas and a happy and prosperous New Year. Christmas Eve and Christmas Day will find many calling long distance to bring Christmas greetings. God sent special messengers to earth to bring greetings that first holy night. He even had an audience all prepared to listen. Hear how he delivered his message.

Reader: Luke 2:8-14

Grade 3: "The First Noel" (vv. 1 and 2)

L: God sends his greetings not just once a year as some of us do at Christmas. Every day he is there to tell you he loves you. Each time we gather in his name, he is present to greet us for he never leaves us. As Jesus stands in our midst tonight, the Spirit speaks words of love in greeting and asks this question through our children:

Children's Chorus:
"Are You Prepared To Receive Jesus?"

Congregation: "The First Noel" (vv. 3, 4 and 5)

(Grade 3 departs and Grade 5 enters dressed as shepherds carrying staffs. If youth need help with the words, attach words to head of staff or the children can make sheep to carry with words on them.)

Time To Prepare Our Tree

L: Some of us go to great lengths in preparing to put up our Christmas tree. We make a family trip to a tree farm or plan an outing in the woods near camp. Just the right tree needs to be selected from among many on the tree lot near the grocery store. Once that special tree has been selected, we place it in a stand and bring out the decorations. Eggnog and goodies accompany our tree-trimming party as Christmas records play in the background or Scrooge is viewed on television. We fuss making sure the trunk is not tilting and trim the branches with garland. Then we step back and pause to ooh and aah over our creation. The shepherds who heard God's greeting that Christmas night did not pause under a tree to gaze at the vanished host of heaven. Having heard the good news hear what they did.

Reader: Luke 2:15-20

Grade 5: "Go Tell It On The Mountain"

L: Christmas proclaims, "Jesus Christ is born!" The shepherds returned home to share that good news with their family and friends. As Christians, God prepares to send us out and announce to the world that salvation was born in a stable. We witness to the fact that the Christ Child, who was placed in a wooden manger, is the Savior Christ, who was placed on a wooden cross to die for the salvation of the world. As Jesus stands in our midst today, the Spirit challenges us to tell others of the Savior of the world and asks this question through our children:

Children's Chorus:
"Are You Prepared To Receive Jesus?"

Congregation: "Angels We Have Heard On High"

(Grade 5 departs and Grade 4 dressed as Simeons and Annas carrying "Praise God!" signs enter.)

Time To Prepare The Faithful

L: God prepares his people to be faithful to their calling to follow him as Lord. He calls to us at Christmas reminding us of his faithfulness in saving the world. Christmas gives us special opportunities to come and adore him. Hear from two faithful servants of God who had waited in patience for that salvation to appear.

Reader: Luke 2:25-38

Grade 4: "Oh, Come, All Ye Faithful"

L: As Simeon and Anna gazed upon the holy infant, they knew in their spirits that this lowly baby was to bring salvation to the world. God allowed them to glimpse the future in that day. They lifted their voices in praise. As Jesus stands in our midst today, the Spirit speaks to our spirits asking this question through our children:

Children's Chorus:
"Are You Prepared To Receive Jesus?"

Congregation: "Infant Holy, Infant Lowly"

(Grade 4 departs and Grade 6 enters dressed as kings.)

Time To Prepare Our Gifts

L: Christmas is a time when we give gifts from hearts of love. We take time in preparing to present to those we love special items which we hope will please them. Wrapping them in colorful paper and topping them with bows, we eagerly anticipate how that gift will be received. God loved the world so much that he decided to send Jesus, his gift, to save it. He sent a star to herald the arrival of the gift and three wise men, who had been prepared through study, saw it arrive. Hear how they responded.

Reader: Matthew 2:1-12

Grade 6: "We Three Kings Of Orient Are"

L: As the kings beheld the perfect light, they presented their gifts and paid honor to the Christ Child. The gift that he would return to them would open heaven's door and bring them salvation. Jesus' body would be laid in a cold tomb and anointed with their gifts. These three friends rejoiced as they beheld the Lord Jesus, and they returned home praising God. As Jesus stands in our midst today, the Spirit presents God's gift of salvation to us and asks this question through our children:

Children's Chorus:
"Are You Prepared To Receive Jesus?"

Congregation: "Good Christian Friends, Rejoice"

(Grade 6 departs and Grade 1 enters dressed as Josephs and Marys with dolls.)

Time To Prepare Our Hearts

L: Advent — a time to prepare: A time to prepare our homes and churches for Christmas celebration. Time to prepare our world to recognize the birth of its Savior. Time to prepare our hearts to be renewed in faith. Time to receive the gift that God offers us in the Holy Child of Bethlehem: Christ Jesus our Lord. In the busyness of the season, God calls us to stop and listen. In the stillness of the night, God calls to us to stop and remember that holy night of long ago as a child was born to a virgin. Hear the story once again.

Reader: Matthew 1:18-25

Grade 1: "Silent Night" (vv. 1 and 2)

Congregation: "Silent Night" (v. 3)

L: Joseph's heart broke when he heard his fiance was going to have a child. "Whose baby was this?" he thought. Mary was so pure, so holy. How had this thing happened?

But God spoke to the heart of this humble man telling Joseph that the child Mary carried was to be the Savior of the world, the long-awaited Messiah. The time has come for us to prepare our hearts for Emmanuel, God with us. As Jesus stands in our midst today, the Spirit touches our hearts asking this question through our children:

Children's Chorus:
"Are You Prepared To Receive Jesus?"

Congregation: "Oh, Come, Oh, Come, Emmanuel"

(All grades reenter and join Grade 1.)

Time To Prepare The World

L: As we have looked at the time taken in preparing our community, our homes, our greetings, our trees, the faithful, our gifts, and our hearts to receive Jesus, we end with the final preparation that only the Spirit of God can perform: preparing our world. God pours out upon us his power to share the good news with others. Hear God's commission to us, his messengers of the Christmas story.

Reader: Acts 1:3-11

All Children: "Joy To The World" (v. 1)

L: God gives us the power to go out in joy to his hurting world and proclaim that the King has come. Jesus, the King born in a stable, will come again to take his faithful, prepared people home. We pray that the message our young people have shared with you today has touched your hearts to respond to your Lord with a yes answer as Jesus stands in our midst again and asks this most important question through our children:

All Children:

"Are You Prepared To Receive Jesus?"

Pastor:

If your answer is yes, welcome the Lord into your heart. If you still are searching as the wise men were for the answers, know God is at work. Let us rise and join in our closing prayer:

***Christmas Prayer:**

All: **Lord, Jesus, thank you for this time to prepare for your birth. Almighty God, we receive the gift of your Son who was born for our salvation. Pour out your Spirit that we may go forth from here today singing our joy and proclaiming the wonders of your love. Be born again in us this Christmas day. Amen.**

***Benediction:**

P: May the Child of Bethlehem bless you and keep you in his love and grace from this day on until his return. Go in peace and serve the Lord.

C: **Thanks be to Jesus, the joy of our world!**

***Congregation:** "Joy To The World" (vv. 2, 3 and 4)

(All grades depart.)

*Offering plates are in the back of the sanctuary. Your gifts of love and appreciation may be shared with our children as you extend your thanks for their preparation of this special Christmas program.